My First Book About Walruses

Amazing Animal Books
Children's Picture Books

By Molly Davidson

Mendon Cottage Books

JD-Biz Publishing

Read More Amazing Animal Books

Purchase at Amazon.com

Download Free Books!
http://MendonCottageBooks.com

Table of Contents

Introduction

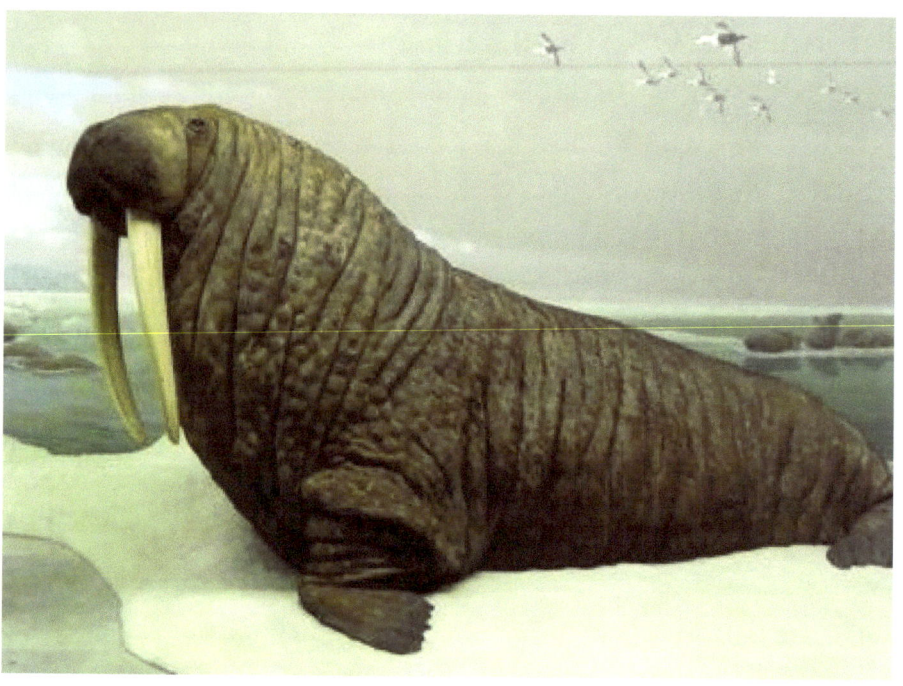

Have you ever wondered about these amazing sea creatures?

Do you want to know why their tusks are so long?

Maybe you want to know why they have whiskers?

What do they eat?

Let's go explore more about this huge mammal that lives in the freezing North.

Information On Walruses

The first thing you may notice on a walrus is its tusks.

They are used for many things. First, they use them to grip the ice in order to pull themselves out of the water.

They also use them to make breathing holes in the ice, so they can breath under the ice while hunting for food.

Lastly, they use their tusks to protect themselves from danger.

Walruses' have rows of whiskers, they use these as sensors to search for food on the dark ocean floor.

They have brownish-red fur all over their body.

A walrus is covered in thick blubber, it can be up to 5 inches thick! This helps keep them warm in the freezing temperatures.

They have front and back flippers. Walruses will turn their back flippers around, so they can walk on all fours when they are on land.

These mammals will spend lots of time in the water. When they are not in the water, they rest on the ice.

The walrus is a very large animal, it is 7 - 14 feet long. It can weigh as much as 3,700 pounds (that's about how much a regular truck weighs)!

There are two types of walruses, the Atlantic and Pacific Walrus.

Pacific Walrus

Atlantic Walruses are smaller, and there are few of them.

The Pacific Walrus are the biggest and they have the longest tusks.

Facts About Walruses

A boy walrus is called a bull, and a girl is called a cow.

A walrus lays in the sun to warm up. This may change their skin from brown to pink, this is a sign they are warm.

When a walrus swims, its skin turns almost white, because of the cold water.

They can stay underwater for up to 30 minutes without coming up for air.

Walruses live in herds of 100 - 1,000!

Walruses do not have very good eyesight, but they have excellent hearing. They can hear another walrus over a mile away.

A walrus can live for about 20 - 40 years in the wild.

Pacific Walruses

Most of the Walruses in the World are Pacific Walruses.

The Pacific Walrus is darker in color and bigger in size than the Atlantic Walruses.

The Pacific Walruses live in the seas to the North of Alaska and Russia.

The walruses travel south in the winter, to the Bering Sea and Siberia.

The walruses travel North in the summer, to the Chukchi Sea in northern Alaska.

Atlantic Walruses

The Atlantic Walruses live in the northeastern part of Canada, and over to Greenland.

The Atlantic Walrus is lighter in color than the Pacific Walruses are, and have a more flattened snout, and shorter tusks.

Baby Walruses

A baby walrus is called a calf.

They can weigh anywhere between 75 to 165 pounds when they are born.

Most of the calves are born in April, May, or June.

A newborn walrus is able to swim from the time he/she is born.

Newborn calves are born with a gray skin and only a small layer of blubber to keep them warm.

The calves stay with their mothers for up to 2 years.

Mother walruses will sometimes keep their calves on their back to keep them protected.

If a bull gets scared it will stampede for the water, sometimes smashing a calf, but if it is on its mother's back, it's safe.

How Walruses Communicate

Walruses's skin is too thick to feel much, but their whiskers are very sensative.

One way they can talk by is touching whiskers.

A mother will teach her baby sounds, that helps them find each other, especially in a danger.

Bull walruses have air sacs in their cheeks which helps them make loud calls, both on land and in the water.

The walruses make many different sounds like clicking, grunting, barking, and whistling.

Another way a bull talks is by being aggressive. He wants to prove he is in charge, so he may throw his body around, cough, roar, and even snort.

Where Walruses Live

Walruses live in icy cold shallow waters close to the Artic Circle.

The walruses like to lay on pack ice or ice floes.

If they cannot find ice, they will rest on big rocks close to the ocean.

What Walruses' Eat

Clams are the favorite food for walruses. In one meal they can eat up to as many as 4,000 clams!

Walruses also eat mussels, oysters, scallops, snails, fish, sea cucumbers, urchins, and starfish.

A walrus will squirt water out of its mouth onto the ocean floor, to uncover hidden food.

Where Do Walruses Come From?

Walruses have triats that are alike with a bear a saber tooth tiger, and seals.

Their front flippers are just like a seals, but their back flippers have five fingers like a bear or tiger.

Walruses need to live where it is cold, their blubber makes them too hot, if its too warm.

Walruses have been around for over a million years.

Seals and Walruses

The walrus and the seal are alike in many ways.

They share the same shape of bodies, and they both swim.

Both seals and walruses move their whole body when swimming, not just their flippers.

Seals nor walruses have ears on the outside of their head.

Seals also have blubber that keeps them warm in the freezing waters of the Arctic.

Seals

Life in the Herd

A herd of walruses need to pick someone to be in charge.

It is usually the bull that is the biggest, has the longest tusks, and is the most aggressive.

Smaller walruses can fight the leader for control of the group.

If a herd is getting too big, a bull and cow may take sereval walruses with them to form another herd.

If you want to know the age of a walrus, measure their tusks. A walrus's tusks will stop growing when it is 15 years old.

If a walrus breaks their tusks, it looses its status in the herd.

Walrus Features

Both boy and girl walruses have ivory tusks.

Boys have longer tusks, and weigh more than the girls.

Their back flippers are a triangle shape and have five bones in them, forming fingers.

In the winter, a walrus's blubber is about 1/3 of their total body weight.

Walruses and Humans

Walruses and humans have come in contact with each other for a long time.

Early on, humans hunted the walrus and the walruses were close to becoming extinct.

People wanted their ivory tusks, they made tools from them, and in order to survive, they ate them.

The only people allowed to hunt walrus now, are natives of the Artic, because they use them for food.

A walrus will not attack, unless it feels threatened.

Since walruses have such good hearing, they get startled when airplanes fly over, and run for the water.

This creates a stampede and many of the young calves or the elderly get trampled.

Airplane companies has started rerouting their airplanes so they don't disturb the walruses, and cause stampeding to happen.

Migration

The Atlantic Walruses, does not move around very much, they stay in the same general area all year round.

The Pacific Walruses have been known to travel over 1,800 miles each year!

These walruses spend their winters in the Bering Sea. During the summer months, the Pacific Walruses head north to the Chukchi Sea, in Alaska.

The baby walruses are born while migrating back to the north for the summer.

Living in Cold Water

Walruses only swim about 4 miles per hour (mph).

For every 8 minutes the walrus is under the water, it will need to breath on the water's surface for 1 minute.

When a walrus is underwater, there is a muscle that will block any water from going down their throat as they open their mouth to breathe.

Walruses lose their body heat 27 times faster when they are in the water, as compared to on land.

They like to keep their body temperatures aourND 98°F, just like a human.

Walruses have been found swimming in water that is as cold as - 31°F!

A walrus warming up in the sun

Walruses Are Endangered

Walruses are considered an endangered species.

The Atlantic Walrus used to be found in Nova Scotia, and sometimes Massachusetts.

Hunting killed many of these walruses, until 1972, when an act was passed to protect them.

Killer whales and poar bears also hunt the walrus for food.

A polar bear on the prowl for food

Something else that harms the walrus, is ice loss. They need to live where it is cold, and they eat animals that eat zooplanton, which live in the ice.

Walruses also live on the ice themselves, so when there is not enough, they have to move, or swim farther to find needed food.

Some laws have been passed that help with slowing down the ice loss, helping all the ice animals, not just the walrus.

Conclusion

We hope you have liked learning all about the walrus.

Next time you go to the zoo (or the Arctic) keep your eyes open for them.

Our books are available at

1. Amazon.com
2. Barnes and Noble
3. Itunes
4. Kobo
5. Smashwords
6. Google Play Books

Download Free Books!
http://MendonCottageBooks.com

Publisher

JD-Biz Corp

P O Box 374

Mendon, Utah 84325

http://www.jd-biz.com/

Mendon Cottage Books

P O Box 374, Mendon Utah 84325